Games for
Physical Education

Games for Physical Education

A teacher's guide

Robin Sykes

A & C Black · London

Published by A & C Black (Publishers) Limited
35 Bedford Row, London WC1R 4JH

First edition 1986
Reprinted 1990

ISBN 0 7136 5527 5

A CIP catalogue record for this book is
available from the British Library

Typesetting by Armitage Typo/Graphics,
Huddersfield

Printed and bound in Great Britain by
Richard Clay Ltd, Bungay, Suffolk

Contents

Preface

It is sincerely hoped that the following pages will give teachers and coaches a repertoire from which they, and those in their charge, will derive many hours of enjoyable and beneficial pleasure.

Physical Education teachers in schools and colleges working with fairly large numbers of mixed-ability pupils can be flexible in their use of the material in this book. They may use the activities simply in their own right, when pitches are unplayable, when taking another teacher's class at short notice, or as a pleasant change from the traditional timetable.

For participants of individual sports, such as tennis, swimming, rowing, weight lifting or athletics, it is hoped that this book will provide a fund of activities from which their club can organise a communal warm-up routine, not only for conditioning and variety, but to foster the sense of belonging to a team.

Remember that whatever the activity, however valuable it may be in affording variety, team spirit or conditioning, it is only a *part* of training and should always be treated as such. Playing touch rugby or relays constantly would do little for any individual team. The real secret lies not just in knowing the activities, but in knowing exactly *when* and *where* to use them!

Robin Sykes

1 Conditioning for Sport and Physical Education

To take part in any chosen sport or even just to enjoy some of the more light-hearted activities in this book one must always remember the importance of *conditioning*. Physical conditioning falls into two main categories:

1 **General**—what was once loosely termed 'getting fit'. This involves, for example, running at various speeds over varying distances, weight and circuit training etc.
2 **Specific**—skills, tactics etc.

Both the above will, of course, take a multitude of forms according to individual needs but, irrespective of format, should always generate:

1 **Enjoyment**—any physical activity should be anticipated with excitement and relish.
2 **Variety**—both in content and location: a change of programme and scene is vital for the maintenance of interest and enthusiasm.

From these two commodities will (or certainly should!) spring that most important of all psychological qualities—**motivation**!

The All-Round Physical Armoury

Anyone actively interested in physical conditioning whether purely for the enjoyment/keeping fit angle or with aspirations at World and Olympic level must, at all times, strive to improve their all-round physical armoury. It is imperative to stress, particularly to youngsters, that mere participation in one's sport or event will *never* improve performance. For instance, footballers who merely play the game all the time will do nothing to cover inherent weaknesses. If they are slow, one-footed or lacking in ball control then they will remain that way until they work on these deficiencies. Similarly, if a tennis player is weak on the backhand an opponent will quickly perceive this chink in his or her physical armour and subsequently play on it. No amount of game-playing will retrieve this situation; consistent and concentrated work on this particular weakness is what is called for.

The components of the all-round physical armoury are:
1 **Speed**
2 **Skill**
3 **Stamina**
4 **Strength**
5 **Suppleness**

Remember, these five components must be tailored to meet *individual* needs and not merely divided by five for each workout. To touch briefly on these aspects:

Speed is largely innate but can be improved with increased strength and flexibility and by working on various speed activities.
Skill in a particular aspect comes after long hours of practice coupled with improved coaching and instruction and is, in essence, the difference between the intended and the *achieved*!
Stamina (endurance) is derived mainly from cardio-vascular work: running at varying distances and speeds to produce what the football coaches would call the '90-minute man'. It forms the basic background ingredient for, amongst others, middle-distance runners but is imperative for *all* sports players.
Strength takes many forms (maximum, elastic, relative, static and so on) but weight and circuit training (carefully planned and supervised) are the two most common methods of acquiring strength. Incidentally, many Eastern European sports coaches and physiologists believe that this is the one aspect of the physical armoury where man can still push himself to greater limits. (The monotonous regularity with which records in weight and power lifting fall and the increasing number of 'world's strongest man' competitions on television is proof of this.)
Suppleness is, from my own experience, the most sadly neglected aspect of all in the physical armoury. A large number of sports coaches are surprisingly misguided in this respect but consultation with any good physiotherapist should soon clear up any misunderstandings.

Warming-Up
The first thing that one must do before any form of physical activity, whether in training or in competition, is warm-up. We warm up for two main reasons, simply:
1 A warm, stretched muscle performs better than a cold one
2 A warmed-up body is less prone to injury
I am constantly amazed at the number of youngsters, in schools and clubs, who dash straight on to the track or soccer pitch with absolutely no form of warm-up whatsoever. Strangely, most seem to get away with this, presumably because they have young, resilient muscles. But this is a dangerous habit to develop and one which can prove costly in later years. Any warm-up depends on the nature and severity of the work to follow and, of course, on the time available. The time spent on warming-up is part of training and preparation, and, since all training is

individual, so, too, is the warm-up. Some people take longer than others. Times can vary from 5-20 minutes but the simple, and obvious, rule is: whatever time it takes for the person to be 'warm, supple and ready for action'.

Mobility and Flexibility

There is a great difference between *mobility* and *flexibility*. We have all, at some time or other, seen, for example, the ugly-looking sprinter with the tight neck and shoulders, restricted arm action and tiny piston-like stride who, nevertheless, outstrips everyone. He may be highly mobile but he is most certainly not *flexible*. Mobility involves vigorous quick movements whereas flexibility involves slow methodical stretching of muscles to increase their range of movement round a joint. Thus, the warm-up session can conveniently be divided into mobility and flexibility exercises.

Obviously, specialist coaches and sportsmen soon devise their own personal warm-ups suited to them as individuals, but for schoolteachers in a class situation the following simple routines may supply a basis from which they can develop their own variations.

Mobility

1   Simple Jogging
Always start with simple jogging to get the circulation going. This should be carefully supervised—simply telling youngsters to jog round the ground or track invariably goes unheeded and results in the usual mass charge at the end to see who comes in first!

2   Exercises
This might include exercises such as deep knee bends, high kicking, arm-circling, trunk-twisting etc. which become increasingly vigorous as the body warms up.

3   A Simple Circuit
This might consist of:
10 press-ups
10 sit-ups   } twice
10 squat jumps

4   Cantering
This can be compared to the jockey who takes his horse for a canter before the race to 'stretch its legs'. If outside, line the class up in extended file, keeping them a metre or so apart, and instruct them to:
1   jog
2   break into a run
3   move up into a fast stride
4   finally sprint to a finishing point
Make sure there is room to 'wind-down' safely (no walls or fences near the finishing line) and instruct them to run in a straight line.

When they reach the finishing line they simply turn round and repeat the process in reverse:

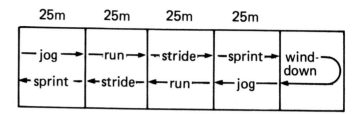

On indoor sessions the 'cantering' may be achieved by running round the gym or games hall and gradually increasing speed on the straights. With fairly large numbers (25-30) this must, again, be carefully supervised to avoid congestion or tripping.

Allow a couple of minutes walking for recovery and the session is ready to begin.

Flexibility

Flexibility exercises should be performed early in the warm up, just after the initial jogging.

The prime example of the advantages of flexibility work is seen in sprinting. Two factors determine how fast a person runs: cadence and stride length. Little can be done for the former since leg speed is largely innate but flexibility work, especially for the hamstrings, can have a great influence on the latter.

Flexibility, however, is just as important, for example, to throwers or participants in racket games where the *range* of muscle work is vitally important. It is important, of course, for *all* sportsmen (how often we see hamstrings injured in the footballer's sliding tackle or stretch for interception of the ball). I have often had soccer and rugby players coming to me to be 'speeded up' (usually young reserve team players trying desperately hard to break into the first team). More often than not, before any speed work can be considered, *flexibility* work is the first essential—of *all* the components in the desired all-round physical armoury (speed, skill, strength, stamina and suppleness) suppleness (i.e. flexibility) is generally the most neglected.

Although flexibility should, ideally, cover *all* muscle groups in the body, the greatest propulsion, naturally, comes from the lower limbs and hence it is here that the majority of injuries occur. Thus, within the context of this book, we may confine ourselves to muscle stretching for the three main lower limb muscle groups.

1   The Calf Muscles

Grasp hold of wall bars or simply lean against a wall. Place one foot in front of the other as shown with the heel of the rear foot raised from the floor. Gently ease the heel down till the foot is flat on the floor. The distance between the feet to begin with depends, of course, on the individual and the condition of his or her muscles. With experience this distance will soon increase as full and maximum stretch can easily be felt on the back of the calf muscles when the exercise is performed properly and the rear foot can be moved further back. Maintain the stretched position for a few seconds then release quickly.

2   The Quads

Hold on to a rail, wall bar or other means of support and, keeping the body completely upright, grasp the ankle as shown. From there push the knee gently backwards (resisting the temptation to lean forwards) lengthening the distance between heel and hip. Hold for a few seconds and release.

3   The Hamstrings

This can be done by individuals but is most effective when achieved with the assistance of two others. The subject lies down, head resting on a cushion or flat on the floor, and raises one leg in the air. One person holds the subject's free limb flat against the ground (hold as shown, not directly on top of the knee cap!) to prevent backward tilting of the pelvis. The subject then clasps his hands behind his knee and pulls the knee close in to the chest, cocking the heel at the same time. The trainer now gently eases the heel upwards and backwards aiming at a point over the subject's shoulder. 30 centimetres (a foot) beyond the vertical indicates a good degree of flexibility. Remember, again, to do the movement slowly and stop *immediately* the subject expresses any discomfort. Always keep the non-stretching limb *flat* on the ground. Change legs as required.

Always bear in mind that these, and indeed *any* stretching movements, must be performed gently and slowly. Jerky or ballistic type movements should *never* be used. Muscles are like elastic bands. Eased gently, they will go to surprising lengths—jerked or pulled quickly they are liable to snap!

Remember, these are merely starting points from which teachers and coaches may develop their own routines: adjusting, adapting or ignoring as they see fit. One final point: although the importance of warming-up properly can never be underestimated, it makes up only the *beginning* of the training session. I have been on coaching courses and in schools where the warm-up is being concluded just as the bell goes! Careful preparation and planning (two basic ingredients of any form of teaching) should ensure this never happens.

2 Minor Games

The following games and relays cater for large numbers of players and generally require little equipment.

1 Zigzag Chase Ball

The object of this game is quick, clean passing of a ball and can be accommodated both indoors and out. Two teams of 5-10 players and a ball each are all that is required. The teams arrange themselves as shown, the players of one team alternating with the other. The distances depend upon the ages and abilities of the players. On the starting signal the balls are passed up and down the line diagonally one or more times, the teams competing to see which can complete the course first. The ball must be handled by each member of the team *in turn* and if dropped must be returned to the player who dropped it before continuing.

   As with many of the games the participants will want to play this more than once. In the first run-through the players will realise that their technique can be improved, and that they want another chance to improve their time or beat their opponents. The teacher can make suggestions if it is obvious that a particular skill is being ignored but it is generally best to allow teams to look for refinements themselves. Some gamesmanship may creep in!

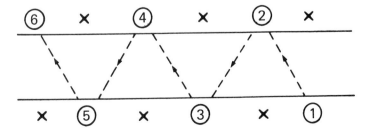

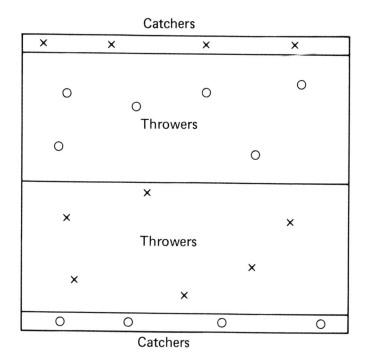

2 Circle Pass-Out

This is best played outside, or in a large sports hall, with teams of 6-10 players and one ball, for example, a tennis or softball. A very good leading-up activity for games such as softball, cricket, basketball or netball, this is a passing and intercepting game, emphasising speed, accuracy and agility.

The central player tries to pass the ball to his or her team-mates in the outer circle which is situated approximately 10-15 metres from the thrower, whilst the defending team in the inner circle (1 or 2 metres in front of the attacking team) try to intercept. The attacking team must move swiftly to 'throw off' the attentions of the marking interceptors in front. They must catch the ball cleanly. This will depend largely on swift, *accurate* despatches from the thrower. After a given time, or a pre-arranged number of pass attempts, the teams change over, the team with the most 'clean' catches being the winner.

3 End Ball

This game is best suited to a gym or games hall, though it can be played outdoors. In the latter, however, much time can be lost with the ball going astray. Two teams of approximately 8-12 members play on a court divided into two equal sections. A further line is drawn 1 metre from and parallel to the back line. The members of each team are divided into throwers and catchers (four catchers, and six throwers is ideal). The catchers position themselves at the back of the court as shown above.

The game is started by the ball being thrown in from the sideline so that it bounces in the centre of the court. The throwers attempt to catch and throw it full pitch to their catchers. Each ball caught cleanly from such a throw scores a point. The catcher then throws the ball back to his throwers who attempt to score again. The opposition throwers try to intercept passes from catchers back to throwers.

Throwers who find their route blocked may pass quickly to better-placed colleagues but the ball may at no time touch the ground. Running with the ball is not allowed and therefore fast running is essential 'off-the-ball' to create more space. Throwers must at all times stay within the limits of their court area. If the throwers or catchers drop the ball, it then goes to the opposing team.

4 Gaining Ground

Although a good outdoor game (especially for distance kicking of a rugby ball), this can be adapted quite easily in a games hall for two teams of up to twelve people using a medicine ball for boys and, possibly, a basketball for girls. The aim is to hit the opposing team's wall (indoors) or to cross their line (outdoors) by powerful throwing or kicking of the ball. Tackling or passing is not allowed and the same player cannot kick or throw twice in succession. Teams take turns to throw or kick, one at a time, trying to force their opponents back. Opposing players must stand at least 2 metres back from players taking their throw or kick and should not bunch together but spread themselves well out to cover the court or field in depth.

A player catching or stopping the ball throws from where it is received and should not try to return it into the mass of the opposition, but should look quickly for space, trying to get the ball as near the opposition's line or wall as possible. As a team forces the opposition back they, naturally, move forward but they should be careful to cover the court or ground behind them since a good, quick field-and-return from the opposition can often lose hard-won ground. If using the rugby ball outdoors, a 'bonus' may be given to a player who fields an opponent's kick before it touches the ground by allowing him, say, six running steps with the ball before returning with his own kick.

Like so many minor games this apparently very simple game offers many opportunities. There is a competitive element although essentially it is fun. The game allows for every team member to play a part. Importantly it is the simple basis for a number of variations depending upon local conditions. Teachers may well like to invite suggestions from the participants for 'rule' changes.

5 Snatch Ball

A speed-off-the-mark game, good for developing agility, this is best played indoors in a games hall, though in good weather, it is just as appealing on grass where distances between teams can be increased

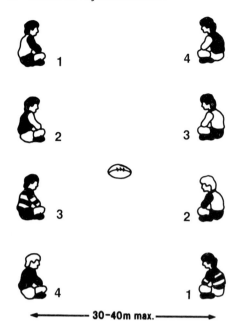

accordingly. It requires two teams of 5-10 players who try to gather up a small ball or other object (a rugby ball or soccer ball is ideal) and return to their own line untouched by their opposite number.

The teams are lined up in sitting positions and given numbers in reverse order. One of the numbers is then called out and the player with that number from each team dashes out in an attempt to snatch the ball and get back over his or her line without being touched by the opposite number. A player cannot be touched *unless he has the ball in his hands*. He may go by any route he likes. For example, he may run past his opponent on the way out as he grabs the ball and may even run over his opposite number's line: it doesn't matter as long as he can eventually get back over his line without being touched. The ideal way, of course, is to get to the ball first, collect it and then get back as fast as possible. The main difficulty is that the collecting player has to change direction and must, therefore, be much faster than his opponent. The ball must be taken cleanly. If it is dropped, the players return to their places after which any other number (or their own again!) is called out.

If both players reach the ball in the middle at the same time the idea is *not* to grab for the ball, and so be touched at once, but to manoeuvre and jockey for possession. They can try feinting movements in the hope of catching the opponent off balance, then snatching the ball away quickly.

The distance between the lines can vary—short distances are often more exciting than long in this game. Also the numbering need not be consecutive in the teams; this will lead to added interest.

6 Running the Gauntlet

Catering for large numbers, this game can be played indoors or out using a tennis ball which is struck either with the fist or a small bat. The object of the game is for the batter to strike the ball and score runs, while the fielders try to hit him or her with the ball. The players are divided into two teams, one batting, one fielding. The fielding team may spread themselves anywhere on court including the area behind the batter. Each member of the batting team goes in turn. The ball must be bowled underhand to reach the batter between shoulder and knee and also at a fair speed in such a way that it can be hit. Whether the batter hits or misses he or she must run. If the batter reaches halfway (i.e. the outward journey person) without being hit, he or she scores one point. At this point the batter may rest but a new batter must come in from the start line. The aim is to get back over the start line to score two points and be able to bat again. A straight out-and-back, of course, also scores the two points. Batters need not run back when the next batter comes in; players may wait over the one-point line until they feel it is relatively safe to run. Obviously it is in their own, and their team's, interest to get back as quickly as possible.

The ball may be thrown at any running player, either incoming or outgoing, by anyone in the fielding team. The fielding team may pass to one another if they wish but they cannot run with the ball. When three people are out the teams change over.

If the ball is caught the batter is out. If the batter is hit by the ball then he or she is out. This game does need careful supervision but is an excellent one for general enjoyment once the players get the hang of it.

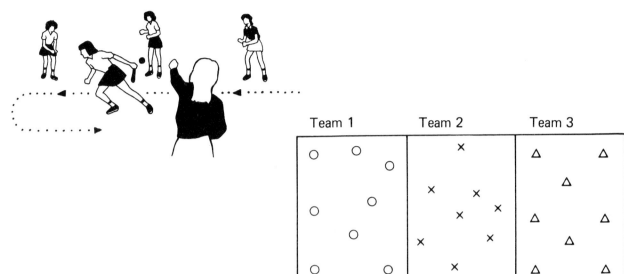

Team 1	Team 2	Team 3

7 Three Court Dodge Ball

A good warming-up or concluding activity, this can be played indoors by any number up to 30-35 using a football or volleyball. The game calls for agility and throwing accuracy, its aim being simply to hit players with the ball. As shown in the diagram, the court is divided into three equal areas and the players into three teams. The object of the game is for the players of the two end teams to throw the ball and hit the players in the middle court. The middle team attempt to avoid being hit whilst remaining within the boundary of their court. The three teams occupy the centre court in turn for a specified time and the team against which the lowest number of hits is recorded is the winning team. The throwing teams may co-operate by passing but no hit can be scored if they overstep their line area or run with the ball.

A simpler method of Dodge Ball is to start with one pupil, who has distinguishing coloured braid, throwing to hit the rest of the class. When someone is hit they put on some braid and combine with the thrower till one person remains. He or she, as the winner, then restarts the next game.

8 Passers Versus Runners

This is best played outdoors and is a test of both running speed and passing accuracy (excellent for basketball , rugby and netball players). One team forms a circle and passes the ball while the other team runs in turn round the circle. The size of the circle depends on the number of players or the amount of running which is required. A soccer centre circle is often ideal. The game starts with the circle team passing the ball around the entire circle, say, six times. They may pass in any direction they wish. Meanwhile the runners run round the circle. Each time a runner comes in the next runner goes. The runners keep running in succession until the passers have completed their circuits (thus runners may go two or three times). Each time the passers drop the ball a run is added to the runners' score. The number of times each runner crosses the finishing line is counted as one point and at the completion of the circuits the total points, including dropped passes, are added up. Teams then change over. Instead of a certain number of circuits the game may, of course, be worked on a time basis.

Although from the diagram and description it seems as if the game must always be a lot of effort for the runners and very straightforward for the passers this is not always the case. The scoring system puts pressure on the passers and as they try to increase the speed so errors creep in. Obviously the game can be adapted for soccer where a loose ball can take time to retrieve.

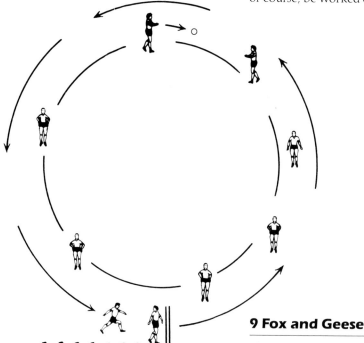

9 Fox and Geese

This may be played by teams of about twelve members, either indoors or out. Players form a line placing their hands on the waists or shoulders of the player in front. The front (detached) player tries to tag the end player of the line who is protected by the dodging and swivelling of his or her team-mates. No breaking of the chain is allowed. Once a player is tagged he or she becomes detached and the previous 'hunter' joins the *front* of the line.

10 Moving Target

A plastic ball is placed between two teams in the middle of the gym. Each member of the team should have a tennis ball or other small ball. At a signal the players throw the ball at the one in the centre, trying to force it over their opponents' line. Players may recover balls from the area between the lines but must retreat to behind their own line before aiming at the ball in the middle. Not *all* the team should be throwers. A certain number should be used as fielders to ensure a constant, *fast* bombardment of the target. Team cooperation is the key to success.

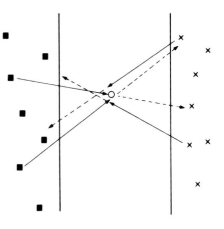

11 Non-Stop Cricket

Best when played indoors, this game requires a cricket bat (or similar), some form of wicket and a hard rubber ball. The ball is bowled underarm and every time the batter hits the ball he or she runs out and round a pre-determined marker and back to his or her batting place. In the meantime the fielding side return the ball to the bowler who can bowl immediately the ball is back in his or her hands, whether the batter has returned or not. When a batter is out he or she lays down the bat and the next player in dashes to pick it up and continue batting. If the ball is in the bowler's hands he or she need not wait for the batter to take up the stance; every time the ball is in the bowler's hands he or she bowls at the wicket. Each 'out and back' journey by the batter counts as one run.

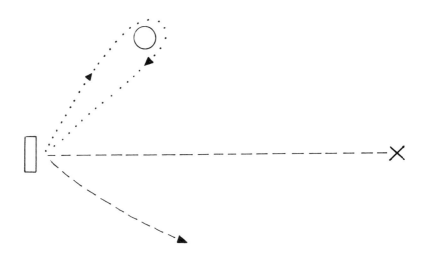

12 Wild Horses

The class is divided into pairs, one of each pair wears some form of distinguishing coloured braid. The latter is allowed to run about freely and, at a given signal, is chased by his or her partner until caught. The last person caught is the winner. Obviously there must be certain limitations on the boundaries—not too far and not too close (where collisions could take place). Half a soccer or rugby pitch is often ideal.

13 Free and Caught

About one-third of the class wear colours. They then chase the others who become 'statues' when caught. Any player not caught can free a 'statue' by touching the hand. The aim is to see which team can turn the others into 'statues' quickest.

The simplest games like this offer a great variety of opportunities to the teacher. Obviously the value lies in general physical warming-up but games such as this promote good group enjoyment because it is clearly fun and not to be taken too seriously. It is also a game where cunning, quickness and even a little modest gamesmanship can be as useful as strength and stamina.

14 Deck Table Tennis

This can be played outdoors by two or four people using a fairly heavy plastic ball. The area to be used is divided into courts. For singles the court should be roughly 10 metres in length and 6 or 7 metres in width. A doubles court should be wider. A bench can be used for a net but it is possible to play the game effectively just with a line drawn across the centre of the court. This is very useful when playing, for example, on the beach providing the surface offers some bounce. Larger numbers can be catered for by arranging courts side by side. Played to the rules of table tennis, this is a game of speed and accuracy emphasising agility.

The server must serve underhand from behind the baseline and the receiver must stand behind his or her baseline until the ball crosses the mid-line before he or she can move into court to play. Rules are exactly the same as for table tennis except that the ball can be hit on the volley to score points (i.e. without having to wait for it to bounce first).

The teacher will have to watch that the rules are altered to suit the situation. In some cases the players will discover ways of ending rallies very rapidly. A two-bounce rule can be introduced or an element of passing between pairs as in volleyball may help. The agility and fun elements should, however, not be allowed to suffer by the introduction of more rules to suit the competitive spirit of players.

15 Gym Squash

An indoor game suitable for a games hall, this is played by two or four people using tennis balls and solid wooden bats. Other types of 'rackets' may be utilised but tennis rackets are too powerful. The object is to win points as in squash or badminton. Players must serve from behind a line as in the diagram. The ball must strike the wall above the 1 metre line. Players are allowed two serves and if both are out-of-bounds service goes to the opposition. After the serve the players hit the ball alternately until the ball bounces twice, rebounds from the playing wall over the line to become out-of-play, hits the roof or the wall below the line. Whoever serves must win their serve to score. Both the front and side walls of a gym may be used. Local rules will frequently need to be introduced.

16 Softball

This is an adaptation of the famous American game. Ideally it should be played outside as a summer game in parks and playing fields though it can be adapted for indoors. There are two teams of 9 people and a referee. A softball, bat and some form of bases are needed.

The basic field positions are shown in the diagram. Distances between bases should be approximately 30 metres and the plate (chalked or marked with sawdust) should be roughly 1.5 metres long and 1 metre wide. The bases are placed in circles approximately 1-1.5 metres in diameter. The pitcher should stand 10-15 metres from the striker and bowl underhand so that the ball passes across the plate between the level of the batter's shoulders and knees. A ball which is bowled correctly but which the batter does not hit is classed as a strike. On the third strike the batter *must* run to the first base whether or not the ball has been struck. If the pitcher throws outside the plate this is classed as a ball. Four of these and the batter may walk to the first base.

If the striker hits the ball into the non-scoring zone neither he or she nor any team-mates occupying bases may run. If the ball is hit twice in succession into this zone the striker is given out. If, however, the ball is hit *anywhere* in the scoring zone, infield or outfield, the player *must* run even if it is a mishit and the ball drops a few feet in front. To get players out, the ball is thrown to the person standing on the base to which they are running. If the catcher holds the ball cleanly with one foot on the base before the incoming runner arrives, then that runner is out. The idea, of course, is to get the ball to first base as quickly as possible each time to prevent progress round to the home base.

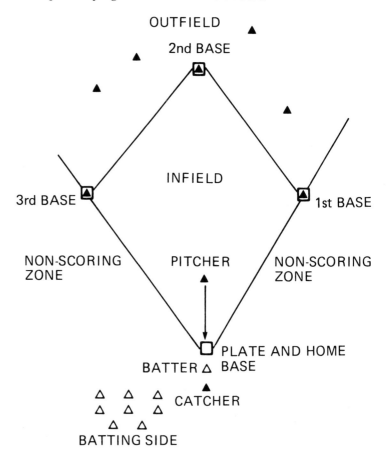

A runner is 'in' at a base if their foot has touched the circle before the catcher at the base receives the ball. Only one runner at a time may be at a base.

Every time a runner crosses the home base, whether from a home run or in stages, one run is scored. If all the bases are occupied, it is sensible to try to get the ball back to the *home* base to prevent the incoming runner from scoring (as well, of course, as getting him or her out). At all other times *first* base is the one to aim for. The innings is closed following a catch (which may be made both in the scoring *and* non-scoring area) or when three people in the team are run-out. On the subsequent innings the player who was due to bat next goes in first.

Players may not run between bases when the pitcher is pitching but only when the striker hits the ball. A player who runs to a base (except first) can change his or her mind and turn back provided they have not covered more than half the distance to the base. If they have, they must run on in the hope that they will get there before the ball or that the person keeping the base will drop it.

In essence the game is similar to rounders but is easier to set up and changes (batting and bowling teams) more rapidly. Adaptions using different bats or balls are useful in certain situations; the above is a general set of rules to act as a guideline.

17 Rider and Horse Tug O' War

This is a variation from the normal simple game of tug o' war and is played by teams of players with partners on their backs. Obviously this is an outdoor game which should be played on soft grass! Simple, boisterous, fun!

18 Watch and Jump

Another useful game with a rope is Watch and Jump. The teacher or coach stands in the middle of a circle and swings the rope round; players have to jump to avoid being hit. This is a good activity for timing and agility.

19 Fire and Water

Participants run freely between benches placed according to space available and the teacher's discretion. On the command 'Fire!', participants must fling themselves flat on the ground. The last one down in this position is eliminated. They then resume running freely. If the teacher calls 'Water!', participants must then dash to stand on the nearest bench. The last person to get onto a bench is eliminated. This entire process continues until the last person in the class, the winner, is left. The teacher may use 'Fire!' and 'Water!' alternately or, preferably, mix them about so that pupils never know which is coming. Two restraining lines at A and B are drawn (or marked) as shown. This is to prevent pupils 'hugging' the benches in anticipation of 'Water!'

The game is ideal for a large class and is best played outdoors on grass. It could be catered for in a gymnasium with non-slip mats but would not, for obvious reasons, be suitable for a games hall with a hard floor surface.

20 Through the Links

Members of the class link hands in columns about 2 metres apart as shown in the diagram. Pupils take turns in pairs, one hunting, the other running and chasing anywhere between the columns. When the 'prey' is caught pupils change places.

The chasing may be made more difficult by making the hunter run in particular directions. For example, in the diagram, the prey may run freely anywhere but the hunter can only run along the columns lengthwise.

Through the Links

3 Relays

Team relays, like the games in the previous chapter, can mostly be played with large numbers of participants and little equipment. The length of time occupied is frequently easy to vary depending upon the number of rounds or repetitions required. Like so many games the first run through of relays can be used as a practice session to enable the players to realise exactly what is required and just how they can perform to their best ability.

1 Boat Race Relay

A 'squatting' relay suitable for teams of up to about eight people, this is a very useful activity for the development of the quadriceps muscles on the front of the thigh so vital in sports such as soccer, rugby, rowing, jumping or basketball.

The teams line up, each member squatting and holding the team-mate in front by the waist. Each team has a leader who stands facing his team and grasps the first member by the hands or wrists. On the signal to commence, the leader starts to walk backwards, the idea being for the team to bounce forward with him in unison until the last person has crossed the predetermined finishing line. A team is disqualified if any member does not squat down properly, stands up, or breaks the chain.

2 Team-Carrying Relay

A good warm-up activity for leg-strength development, this 'piggy-back' racing can cater admirably for large numbers.

Teams line up in file behind a starting line facing the direction of the finish. On the starting signal the second person jumps on the back of the first who runs to the line in front. Having crossed the line the second person drops off and runs back to carry the third person in the same fashion whilst the first person lines up behind the finishing line. The winners are the first team to line themselves up facing back down towards the starting line. The whole process is quite simple: the person who has carried stays over the finishing line—the person who has been carried goes back for the next person.

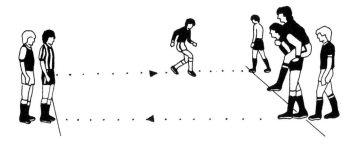

3 Tunnel Relay

This car be played by teams of any number using one ball (preferably a medicine ball) per team.

Teams line up in file with the front person in each team holding the ball. On the starting signal the first player passes the ball back under his or her legs and the ball is then propelled through the legs of all the team who are standing legs astride behind. The last player gathers the ball and returns to the front position where the entire process is repeated. The winning team is the one which has its original starting player back in place first. As a variation, the winners can be the team leading after a certain time, or the team may move forward after the ball has passed between the legs so that the winning team is the one which has all its members over the starting line first. Alternatively the ball may be passed first time between the legs, next time over the top of the head, then through the legs again, and so on.

4 Joining-On Relay

Catering for large numbers, this relay needs teams of 4-6 members.

Marks should be chalked for the first and last players to toe and the teams arranged in lines between the marks. On the signal, the last player runs out to his or her left, round the first player, back across the starting line, then joins on to the player in front (i.e. the second-to-last player in the original line-up) holding him or her by the waist. They then both follow the same route once more, this time with the 'picked-up' player leading. Finally, the first player is picked up, leads over their own line, runs round the back line and returns with the whole team intact to stop once more on their own line. There must be no breaking of contact once players have joined on. The first team back in its original starting position is the winner.

Many relays require that each player performs the same task or runs the same distance as his or her fellow team members. This particular relay does not so it may be worthwhile to change the player's order around if the game is to be played more than once.

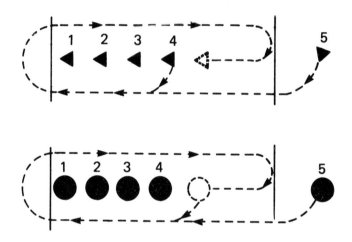

5 Wheel Relay

Four teams of any number are needed for this relay. Teams are formed up as shown. The size of the circle and the number of players can be adjusted according to requirements. The race starts with the first member of each team running in a clockwise direction round the 'wheel' established by the formation of the four teams. Each runner covers three-quarters of the clock, coming in at the tail of his or her own team. In the meantime, each member of the team will have moved up one place. This process continues until the entire team is back in its starting position. The first team back in such a position is the winner.

This relay requires careful balancing of ability amongst teams, otherwise front runners may catch up on the tail of the nearest team. A variation of the game is to introduce the carrying and passing of a ball.

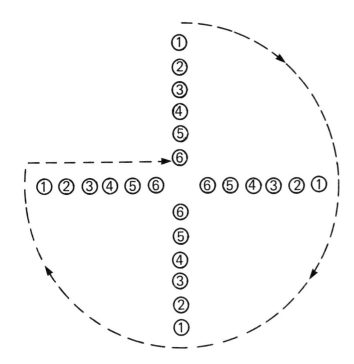

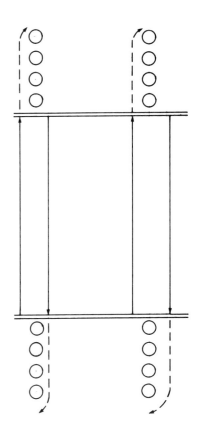

6 Parlaauf Relay

A good general endurance activity for all sports. Teams split into two and line up with one half facing the other. The distance between the two lines is immaterial but, as a rough guide, anything between 30-50 metres is usually adequate. Players decide beforehand from which end the race is to start. On the starting signal, the first runner of each team runs down to their opposite number who then sets off, back in the direction from which the first runner came. Each time an incoming runner arrives the next in line sets off and so on. Incoming runners join the back of their team to await their turn. It is important that participants line up one behind the other in a straight line otherwise collisions can occur between incoming runners and other members of their team who may be standing out of line to see how their team is doing. The race can be run with each runner doing a set number of runs or on a time basis (5 minutes is usually enough).

7 Serpent Relay

Players line up with members placing their right hand back between their legs to be grasped by the left hand of the player behind. The team then runs forward. Again, no breaking of the line is permitted. Of course this style of running can be introduced into other games where group running is required.

8 Centipede Relay

Players stand with their legs apart grasping the ankles of their team-mates in front of them. The idea is to 'waddle' forward with each team simultaneously moving alternate legs. No breaking of the link or standing up is allowed. For a simple idea this is remarkably good fun.

9 Shoulder-Grasp Hopping Relay

Each member of the team flexes one knee grasping the ankle behind him or her while at the same time placing the free hand on the shoulder of the team member in front. Both these positions must be maintained as the entire team hop forward together.

10 Chain Relay

A simple relay where members link hands as shown. Pace judgement for the whole team is vital to avoid collision or tripping with team members in front.

11 Lifting Relay

Teams line up in file with each member of the team sitting on the floor or grass, arms out sideways. The back member lifts the person in front of them on to their feet who, in turn, does the same to the next one, and so on, until the whole team is on its feet. Sitting players must not assist the lifter in any way. The first team standing to attention in its entirety is the winner.

If this game is played very competitively then cheating may occur! The sitting players will assist the lifter. An alternative to try to counter this is to ask the players to haul up their opponents from the front by pulling them upright by holding hands. The sitting players are not allowed to bend their legs but are required to use their heels as a pivot.

12 Pole Relay

Teams line up in file. The first two members of each team then run out to collect a pole (a vaulting pole or a soccer corner flag might be used) laid on the ground some 20 metres in front of them. They each then take one end and run back carrying the pole over their team's heads as shown. When they have cleared the last person they turn round and come back, but this time bringing the pole *under* their team's feet and return it to its original position. They then run back to join the end of their team, the next two runners having gone out to collect the pole and to repeat the process.

13 Bench Relay

Any number of people divided into teams of about eight members can play this simple relay. Each team will need a bench (or similar object) for carrying as shown. Each team begins by sitting astride the bench. On the starting signal they pick up the bench and run, with their legs still astride it, to the turning-round point (which may be a line or wall). The players (not *with* the benches) then turn round to face the other way and repeat the process on the way back. The first team sitting on their benches in the position from which they started is the winner. This is quite a useful exercise for working on leg speed since, obviously, very rapid movements of the lower limbs is essential.

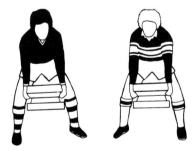

A variation is the 'conveyor belt' relay. The teams carry the bench above their heads pushing it in front as they walk forwards. When the last person loses touch of the bench he runs round to the front of the team. This process is repeated every time the bench passes over the head of the last person. The peeling-off players may *run* but the team must *walk*. The first team over the finishing line is the winner.

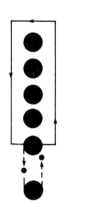

14 Time Ball

This is a running and passing activity good for developing agility and can be played by any number of players divided into teams using one ball (either soccer, basketball, rugby or netball) per team. Teams line up in file approximately 6 metres behind a starting line with 2 metres between each player. Each team has a member who stands on the other side of the starting line facing the team. On the starting signal he or she throws the ball to the first person in the team who, on catching the ball, runs round the back of the team and, on returning to his or her place, throws the ball back to the person in front and then sits down. The thrower then gives the ball to the second member of the team who does the same thing and so on. The last player simply returns the ball to the thrower and sits down. The first team sitting down with the ball in the thrower's hands is the winner. Once they have gone round the back of their team, returning players may throw the ball to their thrower without waiting to get back to their original positions, but they should be careful to 'duck' into their places in case they get the outgoing ball to the next person in their faces!

15 Ball-Carrying Relay

This is a game for teams of any number and requires one ball per team for throwing and catching. It is very good training for games such as cricket, handball, netball and basketball.

Teams line up in file behind the starting line with the first player holding the ball. When the race starts he or she runs to a predetermined line, turns round and throws the ball back to the next in line before moving back a place to allow the next runner to do the same. This process is repeated through the team except for the last runner who need only catch and bring the ball over the line to join the team. The winners are the first team lined up (in reverse order, of course) with the ball in the last runner's hands.

16 Corner Spry

Another game for speed and accuracy of throwing. Teams of 4-8 are needed and a ball for catching and throwing.

Players in each team line up facing their No. 1. When the game starts No. 1 throws the ball to No. 2, who is always on the left. No. 2 throws it back from where it is again despatched to No. 3, and so on right down the line to the last player. When the ball reaches the last player, however, they do not return it but come out to take the place of the leader who then takes the place of the original first player as the whole line moves down a place. This is repeated until each player in the team has had a turn at being leader and the players have worked their way back to their starting positions, with the original No. 1 out in front of the team again. The first team back in the starting position is the winner.

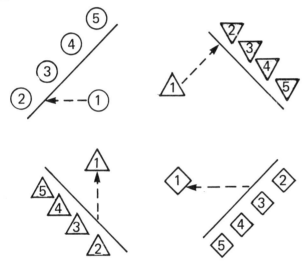

17 Down-and-Back Relay

Teams of any number can play this game, each team requiring a ball of any type according to preference.

Teams line up in file and the race begins when the first runner sprints with the ball and places it down on the ground over a predetermined line. They then sprint back and touch the next runner who dashes out, picks up the ball and brings it back, transferring it to the third player at the starting line. The third person then does the same as the first and so on. It is, therefore, an alternate process of taking down and bringing back. Ensure that the ball is placed down firmly on the ground, otherwise it may roll away, making things difficult for the next runner.

18 Pick-up-and-Pass Relay

An excellent outdoor leading-up activity, this game is especially useful in encouraging young beginners to pass a rugby ball backwards. Teams line up behind a starting line, A. Each team has a passer midway between lines A and B. The relay starts with the passer, No. 1, dropping the ball on the ground or passing it by foot slightly backwards towards his or her own team. No. 2 then runs out to collect, either picking up (rugby ball) or collecting (football), goes past No. 1, then gives the ball back before continuing on to cross line B and sprints back to the end of the team, whereupon the process is repeated. The first team back to its original place wins. The relay can be made continuous by giving every player a chance at being passer. This involves the passer leaving the ball in the middle after the last person has played. The last person then returns only as far as the middle and the relay continues until the whole team has been involved in both passing and running.

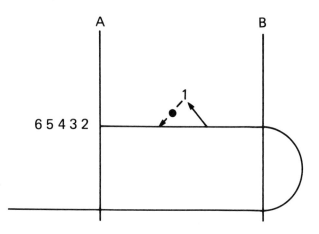

19 Skittle Slalom Relay

Teams of any number can play this game. Each member of the team must slalom in turn through the skittles. To add a test of agility and stamina they must knock the skittles down on the way out and set them up again on the way back. It hardly needs to be stated but objects other than skittles can be used and variations in the relay style can be introduced.

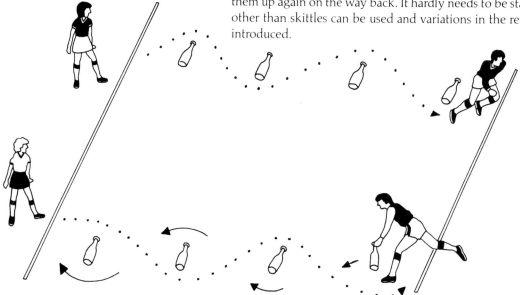

20 Wall-Bounce Relay

Teams line up as shown with a ball. The first player throws the ball up against the wall then dashes round to the back of their team. The second player catches the ball on the first bounce and does the same thing. Each member takes a turn at catching and throwing until the ball is back in the hands of the original first member of the team. As an alternative, the competition may be run on a time basis, i.e. the team leading after a certain time wins. This is a good activity for catching and accuracy of throwing as, obviously, any wild throws or dropped catches from the rebound will spoil a team's chances of winning.

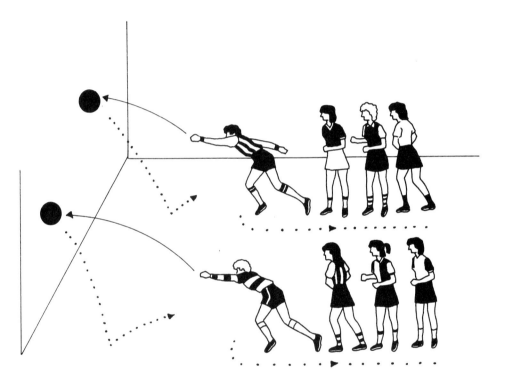

4 Circuits

Circuits in physical education are simply groups of activities put together to aid the participants' physical and skill development. In a circuit a number of activities are set out and the participant approaches them in one of two ways. Either he or she will perform one activity for a specified period of time, noting how many times the task is completed before moving on, or he or she will have a target number of times to complete an activity before moving on. In the latter instance the time taken is noted. Circuits are normally used as part of a general training programme and are hence loosely called circuit training.

Circuit training develops both muscular endurance and cardio-vascular efficiency and is an important part of any aspiring sports player's training. The beauty of circuits is that they can be improvised almost anywhere—home, games hall, gym, spare room or outdoors on a sports field (though, obviously, because of weather conditions it is highly preferable to have indoor facilities, particularly if these happen to include a well-equipped gymnasium!). Also, and this is important for youngsters, it is a *safe* way of gaining strength (as distinct, say, from over-ambitious or even unsupervised weight-training programmes).

The emphasis of this book is on *games* for physical education and not simply training. Circuit training can be arduous and unpopular, especially if the participant doesn't seem to be making much progress. At all levels, but particularly with younger children, it is important to aim for fun and to make the circuits game-oriented even if it is clear to the participants that it is hard work too.

Although it would be wrong to overstate the value of competitiveness in circuits neither should it be underestimated. The game element may be derived from an emphasis on the scoring of circuits with players in teams or operating a handicap system. The popularity of the television inter-town novelty game (It's a Knockout) highlights one approach. The teams can be asked to nominate members to take on one particular aspect of a circuit for, say, double points; this will become their speciality. Teachers may also like to introduce variations using readily available equipment. On hot days a pail of water may be used in place of a medicine ball in lifting games, throwing odd items such as wellington boots can have as much physical value as throwing more recognised objects, and local features can often replace benches and boxes when working outdoors.

General Guidelines for Circuits

1 As a general rule, a circuit shouldn't last much more than 20 minutes, otherwise you're likely to get to the stage where 'dead horses' are being flogged! The timing of individual activities depends entirely upon the participants' needs and the teacher's/coach's knowledge of their ability (see point 5). Similarly the organiser should allow for rests between each part of the circuit.
2 Exercises should, of course, always be in appropriate body segment rotation i.e., upper, middle and lower. Never, for example, have chins-on-the-beam followed by press-ups.
3 Do not have too many exercises in your circuit: six is adequate, eight or nine a maximum.
4 Select the timing of your circuit sensibly. For example, athletes working on a technique session should do their circuit training afterwards as they should always be fresh for technique work. Middle-distance runners going for a steady run, however, can quite easily accommodate a hard circuit, rest for a while, and then go for their run, possibly even doing a further circuit on their return.
5 The duration of exercises sometimes presents problems to coaches or teachers. With a large class of mixed-ability there is bound to be some 'traffic congestion' as the fitter ones catch up, and even pass the less capable. There must be a means of testing progression. The best method is to test each person individually for the maximum in each exercise and then give two-thirds of this number (for example, if the individual can do sixty as a maximum, then he or she can be given forty in the circuit). In this way individuals are working near maximum capacity. As times are reduced and fitness improves simply increase the number of repetitions in each exercise.

As was explained earlier it is important to score the circuit activities to increase the game element and, especially, in more serious training situations, to monitor performance. It is recommended that the teacher supervises this by keeping a score blackboard or by handing out individual score cards.

The chapter is organised with some general ideas first followed by circuits loosely divided into 'competitive' and 'conditioning'. Limitless variations are possible mixing up equipment, sports and methods of organisation.

General Circuits

A few sample circuits might include the following:

Without Gymnastic Equipment

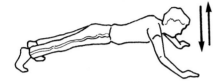

1 Press-ups: Body straight, chin and chest to the floor together.

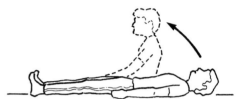

2 Sit-ups: Raise the trunk to the vertical and return (there is no need to have hands behind the neck, do any twisting action or push the head down to the knees).

3 Burpees: From a standing position, drop down into a squat, thrust the legs out to full extension behind, bring them back to the squat, and stand up again. All four movements are done on the one spot. The individual elongated sequence above is for illustration purposes only.

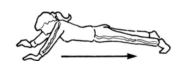

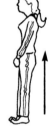

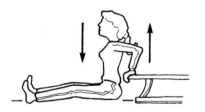

4 Dips on bench: From extended arms, lower hips down to the floor keeping close to the bench until elbows are flexed to 90° angle before fully extending arms again.

5 Back extension: Clasp hands behind neck or back (as shown) before arching the back, trying to look as far back and behind as possible.

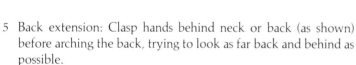

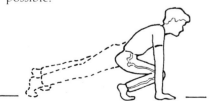

6 Squat thrusts: From the crouch position throw the feet back into full extension before returning to the starting position, making sure that the knees touch the elbows.

With Gymnastic Equipment (1)

1   Chins-to-the-beam or horizontal bar: Overgrasp the beam pulling the body up till the chin clears the beam or bar. Extend fully to the starting position and repeat.

2   Sit-ups with feet under the wall bars: These are the same as the free-standing form described earlier, only this time the feet may be hooked under the wallbars or held by somebody.

3   Deep squat wallbar thrusts: Squat down fully grasping the wallbars as high as possible. From there thrust the body up vertically trying to get the chest as high as possible on the wallbars. On return go back down into a full squat once more. The hands never leave the wallbar they first gripped and the exercise must be performed correctly i.e. right up, right down.

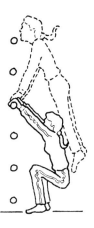

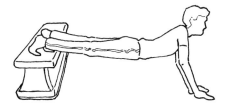

4   Press-ups with feet elevated on bench: This is exactly the same as the normal press-up with the feet elevated to concentrate greater weight (resistance) towards the upper parts of the body.

5   Back extension with feet under the wall bars: As before but this time with the feet anchored under the wallbars or held by somebody.

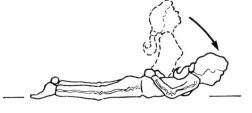

6   Bench stepping or Box-stepping: Have the box at a height where the knee is flexed to about 90° (or slightly more). Extend fully into upright position. Alternate legs accordingly.

With Gymnastic Equipment

1   Step-up on bench with barbell or hard weights: Extend the legs fully as before and change legs regularly. Take particular care in this exercise. The soles of shoes should have sufficient tread to ensure a good grip when placing the flexed leg on the box. Any slipping can be dangerous.

2   Dips on parallel bars: Full 90° bend of elbows then up to complete extension.

3   Abdominal overhead swings from bench hooked to wall bars: From the back lying position on the bench swing both legs overhead to touch the wallbars as shown. Separate the feet as they pass the bench on the way down; this avoids bruising of the heels and also gives added momentum for the subsequent upward swing again.

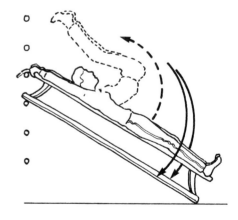

4   Stride jumping on and off bench: This can be performed with or without weights. As with the step-ups with weights, care should be taken to ensure good grip between shoes and bench.

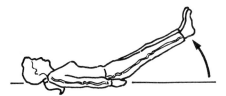

5 Back extension or feet elevation: Raise feet approximately 3-6 inches from the floor, hold, then lower. Weighted discs may be used to increase resistance (place cushion under them to protect the front of feet).

6 Bench-lifting and squatting: Hook the bench on to wallbars at an appropriate height. Raise to full extension above head then lower to full squat.

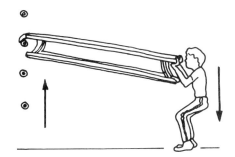

The following diagram illustrates a sample circuit that could be used as a good warming up exercise or as a timed, competitive event (care and supervision should be exercised in the latter).

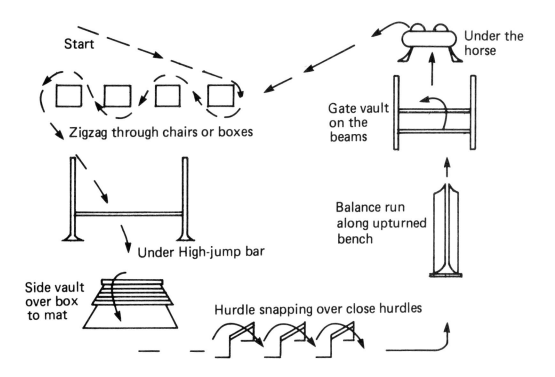

Competitive Circuits for Specific Games

1 Rugby Circuit

A specialist indoor activity catering for 10-15 boys as part of their rugby training, the exercises can be modified according to circumstances, and these can be interspersed with more general circuit activities, but the basic activities are as follows:

1 Players are divided into pairs. One player stands on a high-jump landing mat or similar soft surface holding a rugby ball. The other player runs out from the wall, tackles the player in possession, takes the ball from him and runs to the opposite wall. Having touched the wall he then makes a dive pass to his partner from the mat, his partner having meanwhile taken up position at the other wall, i.e. the starting point. The ball is immediately returned to the player who made the dive pass and the whole circuit begins again with the players now in different positions. Each completed circuit (i.e. after the dive pass) counts as one.

2 One player stands on an elevated object such as a bench or chair. He holds the ball above his head at a height which will make his partner jump as high as he can. The partner jumps up, gets possession of the ball, and gives it back to his partner immediately. Each completed return of the ball counts as one.

3 This is simply passing the ball back and forward over a given distance. Players must stand behind a pre-arranged starting line. If the ball is dropped they must start again. The total completed number of passes between players counts.

4 One player dashes out to a mat, smothers the ball, gets up and returns it to his partner. His partner simply returns the ball to him whereupon he places it on the mat again. He then runs to the wall whilst his partner does exactly the same. Every time a player gets back to the wall one point is scored.

5 This consists of kicking the ball to each other over a buck or horse. Players must stand behind a set retaining line. If the ball is dropped they start again. The number of completed passes is the final score.

Each pair count their points in all the activities and at the end the total points can be counted up to find out which pair are the winners. A scoring blackboard or similar object can be easily devised along the lines of that shown above.

2 Soccer Circuit

Although requiring a fairly extensive range of equipment, this is an excellent form of indoor training for football skills.

Players are divided into pairs, each pair starting at one of the activities, so that the whole class is performing at the same time. Two minutes is suggested for each activity, at the end of which each pair moves round in an anti-clockwise direction. The activities are as follows:

The diagram shows a suggested arrangement of equipment. Participants need to concentrate on their own element of the circuit and not be put off by other activities or footballs that are out of control.

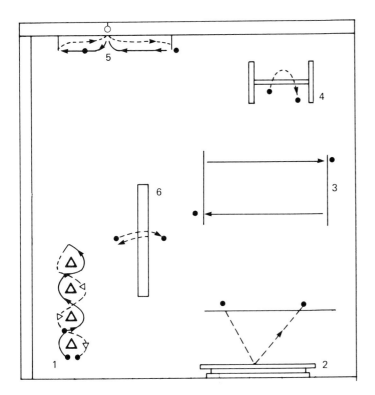

1 Four obstacles (skittles, balls, chairs etc.) are needed. The first player dribbles the ball in and out of the obstacles as shown and returns to the second player who does the same. The ball must be brought over the starting line each time before the next person goes. One point is scored for each completed run.
2 This simply requires a bench turned on its side. From behind a fixed line the pair pass the ball to each other on rebound from the face of the bench. Players must at all times stay behind the line and passes which do not come back over the line do not count. One point is scored for each correctly-effected pass.
3 A simple exercise in the 'weighting' of passes. Two chalk lines are drawn (or one may use any fixed lines such as those of the badminton court) and the pair pass the ball backwards and forwards to each other over the lines. Each time the ball goes over a line counts as one while passes which fall short, naturally, do not score.
4 This needs a beam fixed at a height of approximately 2 metres. Players head the ball to each other over the beam. There is no starting line or any other limitation. The greatest number of consecutive passes counts as the final score.

5   Draw two boundary lines equi-distant from a basketball ring (or improvise by hanging a towel or tracksuit protruding from the wall bars). On the starting signal the first player runs out, jumps up to head the basket, carries on to the line, then turns round and returns heading the basket on the way back. When he crosses the starting line his partner repeats the process. Each lap (out-and-back) counts as one point.

6   Chipping practice over a bench or similar obstacle. To make the practice more difficult the recipient must trap the ball before chipping back. Each chip-and-trap counts as one though these need not be consecutive.

Conditioning Circuits for Specific Games

3 Athletics Circuits

The following are examples of exercises suitable for: sprinting, middle-distance and hurdling; jumping and vaulting; throwing. They can be used as complete circuits or integrated with other, more general, exercises. The teacher should introduce some form of timing so progress can be assessed.

Sprinting, middle-distance and hurdling

1   Back-lying abdominal curl to wall bars: Concentrate on keeping the legs straight and moving slowly.

2   High knee running: This should be done on the spot with the aim of getting the thigh parallel to the ground when in the raised position.

3   Skipping: This ought to be done quickly to see how many times the rope can pass under the feet in one minute or ninety seconds.

4 Squat walking with a medicine ball held over the head: Stay squatting is the key!

5 Alternate high kicks from arm-supported position: Straight legs and 'pointing' toes are essential for maximum benefit.

Jumping and vaulting

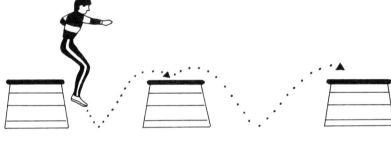

1 Hopping over and between boxes: The ankles must be kept together with jumping; hopping on one leg should be over low boxes.

2 Astride vault over long box: Simple vaulting but supervision on the landing side is recommended.

3 Backward roll into handstand: A very difficult exercise but is good balance work for those who can manage it. Although the aim is to make it in one movement, the less able can usefully undertake the exercise in two parts. A helping hand for the handstand part is useful.

4 Deep squat wall bar thrusts: This is excellent for stretching providing the jump is right up and right down.

5 Upward circle on rings: If rings are unavailable a forward circle pivoting on the waist over a beam can be useful. The aim is both general conditioning and for improved balance.

Throwing

1 Throwing the medicine ball from a lying position: Throw to a friend, sit up and catch the return, lie down and throw again; very tiring!
2 Chins-to-beam: A set number, to be increased, or as many as possible in a set time.

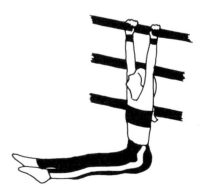

3 Leg-raising from a hanging position on the wall bars: This should be supervised carefully. Ideally the legs should not be bent at all.

4   Press-ups with feet elevated: This is a simple variation on press-
ups that slightly changes the emphasis, making abdominal
strength more important.
5   Back-arching medicine ball throw: The ball must be taken right
back and released before it gets above the head as in a soccer
throw-in.

4 Hockey Circuit

Most of the activities can be carried out in pairs; this represents a good
way of organising the hockey circuit.

1   Dribbling in and out of cones using normal or reverse stick. This
is done as a relay or the whole class following one after the other.
2   Chasing from behind using the long arm sweep to knock the ball
away from opponents.

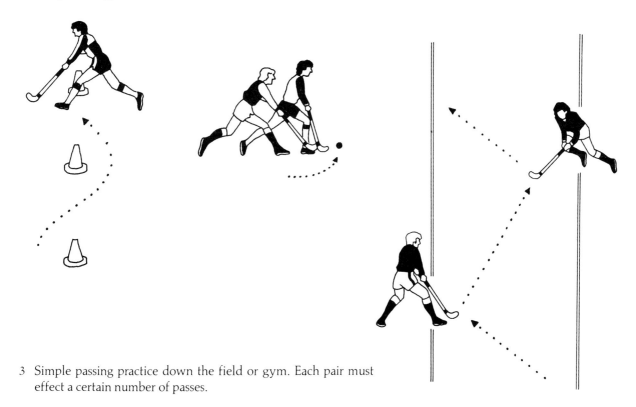

3   Simple passing practice down the field or gym. Each pair must
effect a certain number of passes.

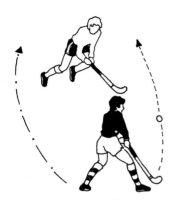

4 Players stand at a specified distance from a partner. Players then run out towards their partners knocking the ball round the right side of them and running round the left. They then collect the ball and repeat the exercise on the way back to their starting position. Halfway through players change positions.

5 Players stand at a given distance from each other. One player then throws the ball and his or her partner stops it, using the stick at the correct angle to effect the action. The ball is returned with a flick, the partner using a hard stop to bring it under control.

5 Volleyball Circuit

This is best carried out by small groups of players. The teacher should stipulate how long should be spent on each activity.

1 Simply keeping the ball up against the wall using either dig or volley.
2 Round the net. Players keep on the move by playing the ball over the net using any shot they like. They then run round to the other side of the court keeping the process going continuously. This encourages control of shot and fitness.

3 Digging practice. Players take turns to go on the mat while others fire steeply-angled shots down at them. Extra players can be used as collectors of the loose ball (see above).

4 Two players feed from the sides giving spiking practice to the others. To encourage concentration and to provide a chance to 'score' a target can be used to aim at (see right).

5 Hopping or running up to reach for a beam or other high target such as a basketball ring.

6 Basketball Circuit

As with other circuits the timing and scoring is left to the organiser. The extent to which a teacher introduces the competitive element is a problem; it may motivate some participants and demoralise others although the aim is obviously to improve an individual score and not to beat other team members.

1 Five consecutive lay-ups from outside the zone. This can be timed or scored by basket.

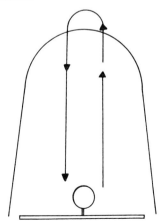

2 Six runs half the length of the court, running backwards in the 'retreating defensively' position.

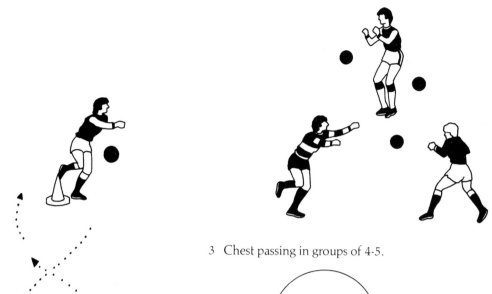

3 Chest passing in groups of 4-5.

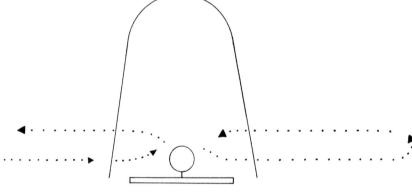

4 Sprinting from wall to wall, jumping up to touch the ring each time.
5 Dribbling through cones using the left hand on the way out and the right on the way back.

7 Netball Circuit

This is best carried out in small groups. Teachers should stipulate how long to spend at each activity.

1 Possession ball over selected area of the court.
2 Shooting competition from varying distances and with or without defender intervening.
3 Passing practice up and down the court.

4 Bench "basketball" with attackers playing defenders. The player on the bench is the pivot for one team and has to take passes from each of the attacking teams in turn.

5 Leg-strengthening work on boxes. Remember to supervise the landing area; those participating may be quite tired.

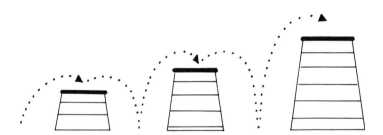

5 Exercises and Activities Relating to Major Games

General Conditioning Activities
1 Pursuit Race

An excellent concluding activity for track sessions which caters for any number of runners round a track or other courses (for example, soccer pitches or forests). The aim is to complete the course without being overtaken.

The runners line up in single file, with the better performers to the rear. The coach or teacher taps the first runner on the shoulder as the signal to run, then starts the others at chosen intervals until they are all running at the same time. The idea is to pass the runners in front but not be overtaken by those behind (a good test of pace judgement!). Pass but don't be passed! Overtaken runners drop out and return to the starting line leaving those who finish the course as the successful runners. To discourage runners from agreeing not to overtake an elimination method can be introduced. You must overtake one runner to proceed to the next round.

2 Obstacle Course Relay

A good all-round relay incorporating a variety of track and field activities, this is best as an outdoor activity and also requires a fair amount of equipment and planning. A typical course is laid out in the diagram. The numbers refer to the following obstacles:

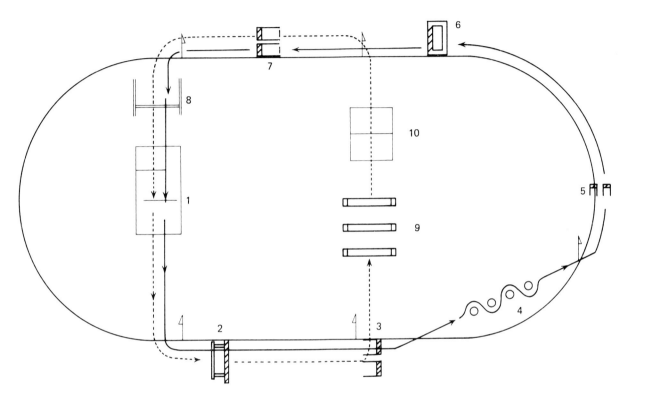

1 The starting point. Two or three high-jump or pole vault landing beds placed together lengthwise.
2 Steeplechase barrier
3 Two hurdles
4 Four obstacles (such as chairs)
5 Two hurdles
6 Steeplechase barrier
7 Two hurdles
8 High-jump bar approximately 75 centimetres in height
9 Three benches
10 One or two high-jump landing beds

The single line represents a full lap, the dotted one a shorter route for youngsters. Whether participants go over or under obstacles is up to the discretion of the teacher or coach. Teams line up at the side of the starting point (1) and the outgoing runner leaves when their hand is touched by the incoming runner who, in this circuit, can gain distance by a headlong dive across the mats (most children love this bit!).

The course can be altered or adapted according to the needs of the teacher or coach and a variety of alternatives can be employed. For example if in the vicinity, horizontal jumping pits could be utilised (hopping through the sand) or three or four hurdles could be laid out in succession as in a race. Part of the course could be confined to hopping or continuous standing broad or triple jumps.

The diagram above illustrates a fairly extensive course; the following a simpler one.

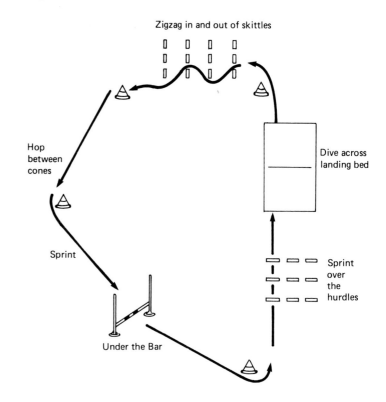

3 Assorted Activities

This is an ideal competition for a large class (30-50) in a normal gymnasium using basic gymnastic equipment. The class is divided into six groups, each group attempting to get the highest possible score within the space of 2 minutes at their own particular activity. They then move on in a clockwise direction to the next activity and so on until the complete circuit has been covered. Scores are recorded on a blackboard and final placings arranged accordingly. A typical course is laid out in the diagram.

1   The group forms a circle and passes a medicine ball round as many times as possible.
2   Each player travels along the beams using overgrasp, jumps off, runs along the bench and returns to end of queue. Each completed circuit counts as one point.
3   Players lie on their backs with their feet tucked under wall bars and doing as many sit-ups as possible within the 2 minutes.

4 The bottom section of a box is lined up against the wall. The team stands behind a fixed line and each member kicks the ball in turn trying to get it to rebound from within the section. Each shot on target scores one point.
5 Each player goes over and under the two bucks and back along bench. Each circuit scores one point.
6 This is a broad jump from a standing position. One point is scored for an average jump, two for a good one and three for the furthest box. Distances are at the teacher's discretion. The group takes as many jumps as possible in sequence within the allotted time.

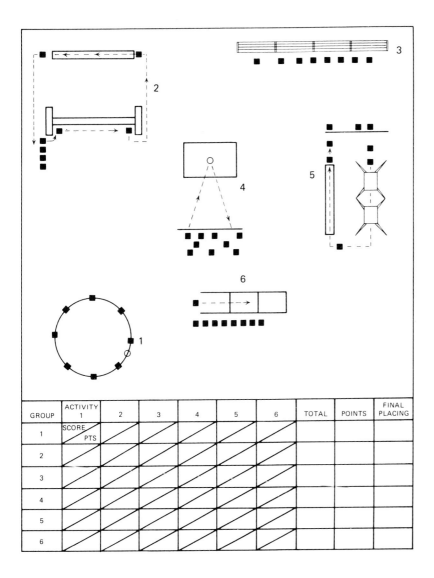

GROUP	ACTIVITY 1	2	3	4	5	6	TOTAL	POINTS	FINAL PLACING
1	SCORE / PTS								
2									
3									
4									
5									
6									

4 Back-Lying Sprint Competition

A speed-off-the-mark activity, good for developing fast reactions and agility. Participants lie flat on their backs with their heads touching the starting line. On the starting signal they get up, turn and sprint to a finishing line some 20-30 metres in front of them. Ensure that there is plenty of space between each runner and that they run straight to the finishing line and not to teacher or coach. This can be made quite exciting by organising a sort of mini-Olympic sprint competition: the first, or first two players go into the semi-final and the first three in each semi-final go into the final; and in the final, the winner takes the gold, second the silver, and third the bronze. In this way competitions can be turned over quickly ensuring plenty of competition for all.

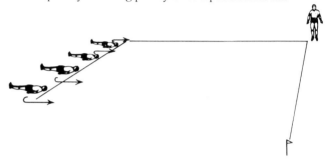

5 Diagonal Sprinting

Four flagposts are arranged as in the diagram. The recovery jog distance should be about 30-50 metres and the distance between the two parallel jog lines about 60 metres, depending, of course, on the size of the class or squad. The process is quite simple: players follow the lines shown by the arrows—each time a player runs diagonally they sprint, each time they run on the parallel lines they jog. Careful supervision is sometimes required as the 'head' often catches up with the 'tail' in this activity, especially at the centre of the sprint 'cross'.

6 Hops to or through the Pit

Although a specific activity for horizontal jumping (long or triple jumps), this is an excellent leg conditioner for *all* sports. A jumping pit and runway is needed. From a standing position the player first hops from the beginning of the sand pit through to the other side counting the number of hops it takes. They then move back to the start of the runway and do the same thing again counting the number of hops, this time from the start of the runway, till they reach the sand. In both cases the player is *always* striving to reduce the total number of hops required.

7 Indian Trail Running

The squad jog round the track or circuit. Each time the teacher blows a whistle the last member of the file sprints up to the front. The whistle should be blown fairly quickly and regularly to ensure frequent activity. The pace of the 'jog' should also be watched; sometimes the leading group tend to run too fast making distances increasingly difficult (and tiring!) for those at the back.

8 Thirty-second Run

A simple test of speed and endurance, this can be accomplished indoors or out and is quite good for assessing possible middle-distance potential in young schoolchildren. The aim is to run as many lengths as possible of the games hall backwards and forwards within a 30-second period. The class is divided into groups of 4-6. Distances are calculated to the nearest quarter of a length. It can be run on a 'one-off' basis to see who covers the most distance or on a 'knock-out' basis with, say, the first two in each heat going into a final.

9 Longest and Shortest Strides

This is largely an individual activity good for leg speed and stride length.

Ask players to run 30-40 metres using the longest possible strides they can, in other words, trying to cover the distance in the smallest number of strides. Then ask them to run the same distance using the shortest possible strides, in other words, trying to use as many strides as they can. Always have these distances timed otherwise the runner may end up taking gigantic bounds (overstriding) or conversely running on the spot. The aim is to try to improve stride length and leg speed.

10 Changing Direction

A very simple chasing game played in pairs in which one player chases the other, trying to 'tag' him or her by touching. The person being chased, meanwhile, swerves, dodges and sidesteps to avoid being touched. A time element may again be introduced to make the activity competitive. It is best to confine limits to within a certain area (for example, the rugby 22 metre line, the soccer penalty area or the hockey 'D') otherwise it might turn into a long distance run!

Like the two 'games' above this may seem hardly worth describing at all. However it is surprising just how much enjoyment and benefit can be derived from such a simple activity. The teacher or coach is shown to be introducing new elements to lessons or training, the chance to practice a new skill (albeit a simple one) is offered to the participant and the exercise itself can be as physically demanding, and thus as beneficial as other more traditional elements. What has been mentioned before, and what cannot be over emphasised, is just how much the success depends upon the organiser. To play a game like this 'cold' will not be very productive. To play upon local pecularities, the participants' idiosyncrasies and the dynamics of the group involved are all essential. The teacher's or coach's own personal involvement may also work wonders.

11 Up the Clock and Back

A simple continuous running activity. Each person runs out (for example, in a lane of a track) with, or without, a ball, for a distance of 30 metres, turns round, returns to the starting line and then goes 50 metres, 70 metres and finally 100 metres. They then repeat the process in reverse—i.e. 70 metres, 50 metres, 30 metres and back to the finish. The runs can be done as shown or in one lane.

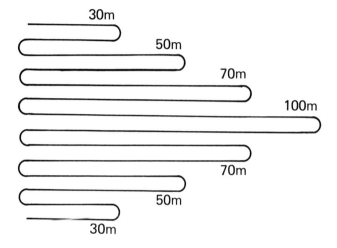

12 Continuous Relay

A relay round the track in teams of anything from 5-8 members. Runners hand over the baton and *wait there* till the baton comes back to them again. In other words, it is a continuous process. Usually 3-4 laps is sufficient.

13 Shortened Fartlek

An abbreviated form of the middle-distance runner's training, this involves running at different speeds over varying types of ground. For those with limited facilities who do not have access to terrains such as forest paths, this can be improvised within school grounds; in this case it would be worth the effort to get the runners to go through sand pits, around trees, over rough grass etc. The emphasis should be on variety of both speed and terrain. The following is a brief sample of what might be used:

1   a jog round the area
2   a few easy strides to the halfway line
3   some short runs up any incline
4   a few sprints across the penalty area or 22 metre line
5   5 minutes jogging
6   two runs the length of the pitch at three-quarter speed
7   a few more speed bursts
8   5 minute jog to finish

14 Sprint Relay on a Square

A very simple relay (with or without a ball) where the stages are round a square instead of a track. The running strengths required are different from those needed on a normal track while the course itself is easy to construct.

Skill Practice Games

1 Watch the Hare

A useful practice for any activity which involves speed off-the-mark (soccer, rugby, cricket, hockey, badminton etc.). To prevent congestion or accident it is best played in pairs. The two players stand behind a starting line facing the front whilst the teacher stands behind them with a ball in his or her hands. The ball is then thrown out to the front and the one who gets to it first is the winner.

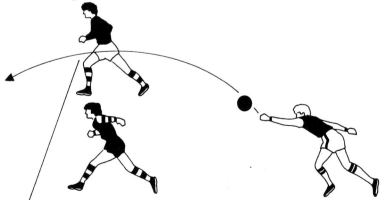

2 First to the Ball

Another activity along the same lines as the above. Two restraining lines are drawn approximately 20-30 metres apart and the teams line up at each end with a rugby or soccer ball in front of them on the opposite line. (Note, the teams are not facing each other *directly*.) The teacher stands at the end between the lines and on their command the first player dashes out to see who can reach the ball in front first, each player in the team subsequently getting their turn. The activity can be made 'specific' by having the soccer players, for example, trying to dribble the ball over their opponents' goal line or the rugby players 'scooping' the ball off the ground into a pass. This can also be usefully adapted for hockey.

3 Chasing the Attacker

A practice for getting quickly back into defence applicable to most ball games. A player, or players, give the attackers a start then set off in pursuit to try to prevent them scoring, whether it be a goal, basket, try, etc. One aspect of this game is the panic experienced by the attacker. As he or she is pursued by the defenders the need to aim for the goal or basket is heightened. This often results in missed opportunities and, as such, closely reflects real match situations.

4 Speed across the Circle

An exercise in speed useful for hockey and soccer players. Players form up round a circle (a soccer centre circle is ideal), one player with a ball at his or her feet. To start the game they dribble the ball across to another member of the team (not the one next to them), give them the ball then take their place. The recipient repeats the exercise with another player and so on. Competition can be introduced amongst teams by seeing, for example, how many runs/deliveries can be made by each team in a certain time. This can also be adapted for rugby players who carry and pass the ball.

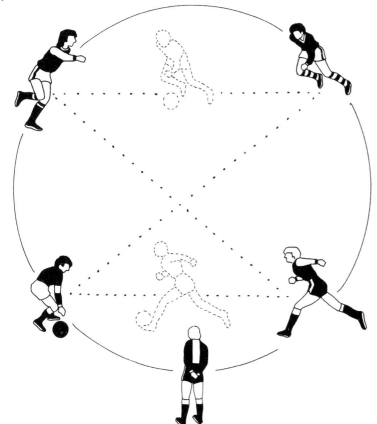

5 Reaction

A group of participants form a circle around a central thrower who has a tennis or softball in their hands. The central player is to throw the ball to the catchers on the ring. Plenty of space should be left between players. All players have their hands behind their backs and must only bring them to the front to catch the ball. The thrower may feint to throw without actually letting the ball go and catchers are eliminated if they move their hands from behind their backs. Any player dropping the ball is also eliminated. Throws should become increasingly difficult as the field narrows to ensure a quick turnover of games. An umpire is a useful addition to ensure that throws are fair.

For young players at primary school (or if the teacher wishes to make the throws fairly difficult) the rules can be changed so players don't have to place their hands behind their backs. Another form of the game is to have the catchers with their backs turned to the thrower who shouts as he or she releases the ball. Since there will be no exact indication as to whom he or she has thrown, all players must turn round at the same time in the hope that, if the ball has been directed to them, they will respond quickly enough for a clean catch. This is quite a popular goalkeeping practice on an individual basis.

6 Pass and Squat Relay

A simple speed and accuracy of passing game. Players line up in file with a thrower in front. He or she throws the ball to each member of the team in turn who returns it before squatting down to permit the ball to pass over his or her head to the next player in the line. The last player merely returns the ball to the thrower and the first team squatting down in its entirety is the winner. This can be performed with heading or using specialist throws from basketball or netball.

7 Hurdle Relay

A straightforward 'out-and-back' relay using hurdles and a ball in which, for example, rugby players could carry the ball while jumping the hurdles. Soccer players push the ball under the hurdle before they jump over them.

One point about this apparently simple game is the way in which the teacher can utilise, say, five hurdles in a large number of ways. Following from general athletic exercise the hurdles can be used to develop skills for a number of sports. The range of games shown to be possible may encourage the participants to experiment with their own variations. It is not necessary to have a lot of equipment or even a large number of people to put together useful and enjoyable games.

8 All against All

This form of 'Dodge Ball' (p.19) is an indoor activity for a games hall and a large number of participants. Half a dozen or so tennis balls are thrown into the class for players to pick up and throw, creating a 'free-for-all' situation in which anyone hit with a ball is eliminated, the last person remaining being the winner. Running with the ball is not allowed and players who *cleanly* catch a throw directed at them are still left in the game. Be careful about the rules in this one. The target zone should be spelt out and no participant allowed to throw the ball at the head of others. Softer balls than tennis balls are useful.

9 Simple 'Keeping it Up'

This is suitable for games such as volleyball or soccer. Teams try to keep the ball off the ground, using their respective team skills, for as long as possible.

Teachers and coaches should never shun the opportunity to formalise games that children (and adults) play in a casual way on the beach or in the park. A couple of rules introduced and the supervision of the session by the group leader—who keeps score too—will keep the participants involved for a long period.

10 Numbers from the Left or Right

This activity offers useful practice in developing skills for football or hockey. It requires a relatively small pitch (say, the penalty area) with two small goals at either end. Teams of players stand behind the goal at both ends. The teacher then calls out a number and side, i.e. one from the left, three from the right etc. The corresponding number of players from each team come round from the appropriate side and attempt to score against their opposite number. They may do this any way they like, shooting on sight, passing and tapping in, or dribbling individually. Once the ball goes out of play they form up again with their respective groups on any side of the goal they wish.

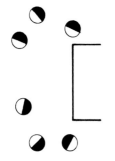 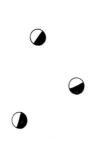  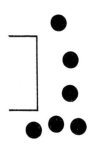

11 Speed Passing

This game can be adapted to many sports: hockey, netball, football, rugby or basketball. The following example shows how it is used in rugby.

Teams of 4-5 pass the ball up and down the pitch to see which team covers the entire pitch length in the fastest time. To prevent one series of passess along the line and then a straight sprint by all players to the finish, the ball must be passed back and forwards along the line at least four times.

The time is counted from when the first player on the left crosses the starting line till the last man in possession crosses the finishing line. Forward, or dropped, passes result in disqualification.

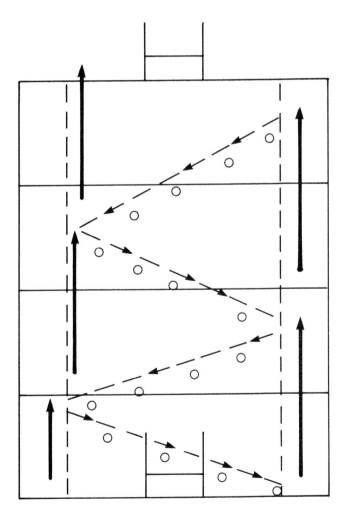

6 Mini-Games

1 Head Handball

A superb activity for any team, this is best played by two teams of 6-8 players playing outdoors across the width of a section of a rugby or soccer pitch or indoors in a games hall. The object is to pass a soccer ball by hand at speed so that it can be headed into the opponents' goal—emphasising in the process intelligent use of space and speed both on- and off-the-ball.

The ball should be moved very fast end-to-end using rugby or basketball passing techniques. The successful teams will be those who make the most intelligent use of support, dummy runs and positional play combined with fast, sensible running.

Only three strides are permitted with the ball before it must be passed. The ball cannot be pulled from a player's arms by opponents who must gain possession by means of interceptions, saving shots at goal, loose balls running free, or by their opponents putting the ball out of play.

A goal is scored by heading the ball into the opposition's goal either from a colleague's pass, a deflection, a rebound or a loose, bouncing ball. Players may not throw the ball up to themselves for heading. Anyone may save a shot—there is no goalkeeper as such. At no time may the feet be used except in *blocking* (not kicking) the opposition's headers at goal when on the goal line. Infringement in this respect results in a penalty header for the attackers. In this case, the ball must be thrown to the taker by a member of the team.

Playing time should be carefully regulated. As players tire and slow down the real value of the game deteriorates and when it is veering towards walking pace it is time to finish. The game is at its best as a concluding activity for all types of team game.

2 Soccer Tennis

This game is suitable for two teams of 4-6 players and can be played outdoors on a calm day or otherwise indoors in a games hall. It is, obviously, very much an activity specific to football. A light, plastic ball is better although a football can be used and the court divided by a net or other similar barrier. The teams try to score points by playing the ball to their opponents' court in such a way that it cannot be returned.

Each member of the team serves the ball in turn from anywhere behind the baseline into the other team's court either by heading, chipping or bouncing it, then kicking it over. It may fall anywhere within the court and may be returned on the volley or after one bounce, but not more. The ball may be returned by the use of head, foot or knee but hands are not permitted. The scoring is the same as in badminton, i.e. only when serving can a team score a point.

3 Crab Football

Two teams of 6-8 can play this indoors in a gymnasium or outside on grass in dry conditions. The aim is to score goals with a football using soccer techniques but keeping hands on the ground.

Players must adopt the 'crab' position and may only play the ball in this fashion. They can move as fast as they like by pushing with the hands and sliding the seat along the floor, or by raising the seat and travelling on hands and feet. At least one hand, however, must always be in contact with the ground. Goalkeepers may adopt the kneeling position and are the only players permitted to do this. Indoors, mats should be used for knee protection. Infringements result in free kicks. Throw-ins, goal kicks or throw-outs may be taken if boundaries are used. In the normal school gymnasium it is usual to make play continuous by allowing the ball to remain in play when it rebounds from the walls.

4 Touch Rugby

A fantastic activity for all team games as well as a first class conditioner, this can be played indoors but is best outdoors on a pitch (whose size is dependent on the number of players) simply marked with four corner flags. The object is to carry the ball untouched over the opposition's goal line. There is no need, unless so desired, to touch the ball down.

The ball must be kept off the ground at all times and should be passed out in a line similar to the actual game of rugby itself. It is best, except at very young level, to insist on passing the ball backwards. This avoids players standing up near their opponents' line and players getting mixed up with one another. If a player in possession is touched or his team drop the ball, then the ball goes to the other team.

To restart after an infringement, the team in possession should line up across the pitch behind the player with the ball who passes the ball out. Meanwhile the opposing team should retire at least 5 metres to allow the team in possession to get going. There is nothing to stop a player passing immediately to one of his team-mates before any line up if he feels there is an advantage to be gained by this. Players should run hard with and without the ball. If the line ahead is clear players should go for it because, even if caught, the team as a whole is now nearer the other team's line. Backing-up is essential because if a player is about to be touched he can do nothing but pass the ball. Kicking is not allowed. Avoid bunching as this makes defence easier for the other team. Players should spread out, pass the ball about, try to find space and, above all, in both defence and attack—run!

A variation is two- or three-touch rugby where a team may keep possession for two or three passes after which they must relinquish the ball to the opposition.

5 Team-Carrying Soccer

A very simple game played to soccer rules in which players must carry other team members on their backs. It is advisable to change over frequently. This is a conditioner for the leg muscles, but obviously it should be carefully supervised, and the time regulated. It should be played on a smaller than usual pitch, with resulting rule modifications. Changeovers can take place as frequently as required but players may only play the ball when carrying a team mate.

6 Mobile Goal Game

A good game for developing skill and agility, this can be adapted to suit many sports: basketball, rugby, soccer, hockey, handball or netball. The object is simply to get the ball through the goal which is carried by one player of each team. These players try to manoeuvre the goal to permit scoring by their own team or prevent scoring by the other team. The carriers must not let the pole go. If they do, a point or goal, is awarded to the other team. To add excitement to the game, a number of balls can be introduced.

7 Five-a-Side Soccer using a Rugby Ball

This sometimes adds a little variety to the usual abbreviated soccer game and, as the players will soon discover, a certain amount of frustration!

8 Bench Basketball

Two teams of 4-8 people are needed for this game which is best played either in a games hall or outside on a hard court. It is a variation of basketball and emphasises passing and intelligent use of space. The equipment needed is a basketball or netball and two benches, chairs, or boxes.

Each team has a member standing on the bench at their opponents' end of the court. The idea is to get the ball cleanly into this player's hands, a point being scored each time this is effected. He or she may move anywhere along the bench to take a catch but can not come off it. Normal basketball rules apply as regards dribbling, carrying, passing etc. As a variation, the rules which apply to head handball or netball may also be used here.

9 Bouncer Handball

This can be played on a hard court, inside or out, ideally by two teams of 4-6. Larger numbers tend to cause congestion and leave too many players not sufficiently involved in the game. The aim is to bounce a mouldmaster or heavy, plastic ball between goalposts. The pitch should be approximately 35 metres by 25 metres. This is another good conditioning game, again encouraging intelligent use of open space and speed off as well as on the ball.

Players may keep possession by running and bouncing (basketball style) but may not run with the ball. A player must always pass immediately he is touched by an opponent, if not the ball goes to the opposing side. Players may not obstruct or overguard but may gain possession by interception or fair tackle (blocking, dispossessing whilst on the move etc.).

A jump ball is the outcome if two players get the ball at the same time. If a team puts the ball out-of-play, the opposition take a throw-in. When a goal is scored the game is restarted from the centre by throwing the ball up between two opposing players.

10 Possession Ball

A simple but effective game. Players of one team simply try to pass the ball (rugby, hockey, soccer, basketball, and even volleyball and cricket) amongst themselves, retaining possession and keeping it away from their opponents as long as possible. Obviously to do this they must not only be accurate in passing but must run to create space and get away from their opponents who should be chasing everywhere to intercept and gain possession. The winners can be either those who make the highest number of consecutive passes or the team who hold on to the ball for the longest period of time.

The area of play needs to be defined and the umpire has to decide how long a player can hold the ball before releasing it.

11 Seven Versus Five Netball

In this game, seven players with the ball take on five. The seven try to get the ball quickly up to their shooter across each of the three zones in turn, as the normal rules of netball stipulate. The five must cover space, while the seven move quickly to counteract this by capitalising on their two extra players.

12 Passing and Shooting Netball Practice

Two teams of a chosen number (usually between 5-7) try to pass the ball ten times amongst their own team without interception from their opponents, normally within the confinement of a half-court. When this is achieved, each member of the team is allowed a free shot at the net from anywhere within the shooting zone. Every player who scores earns their team a point. The game can be played either on a score basis (first team to twenty) or on a time basis (5-10 minutes depending on circumstances).

7 Checklists

The following checklists provide an 'at-a-glance' guide to the games in this book. They are designed for the busy teacher or coach who has little time for planning training sessions. They are, however, by no means definitive, and can be adjusted or adapted to suit the requirements of each individual.

Checklist 1 is a handy reference guide to the games, outlining their basic components. The times (in minutes) and numbers of players are simply recommendations. *Checklist 2* shows how the games can be best utilised in connection with specific sports.

Checklist 1

Game	Page	Players		Equipment	Location		Duration	
		Min.	Max.		In	Out	Min.	Max.
Zig Zag Chase Ball	15	10	40	Ball	In	Out	5	15
Circle Pass-Out	16	12	50	Ball	In	Out	5	10
End Ball	16	16	24	Ball	In		10	20
Gaining Ground	17	10	24	Ball	In	Out	10	20
Snatch Ball	17	10	40	Ball	In	Out	5	15
Running the Gauntlet	18	10	40	Ball/Bat	In	Out	10	25
Three Court Dodge Ball	19	15	30-35	Ball/Distinguishing braid	In		10	25
Passers v. Runners	19	10	40	Ball		Out	10	20
Fox & Geese	20	6	30-35	—	In	Out	5	15
Moving Target	21	8	40	Plastic Ball/Tennis Balls	In	Out	5	15
Non-Stop Cricket	21	10	20	Bat/Ball/"Wicket"	In	Out	10	40
Wild Horses	21	20	40	—	In	Out	5	10
Free and Caught	22	10	50	Colours	In	Out	5	10
Deck Table Tennis	22	2	20	Fairly heavy plastic ball	In	Out	10	30
Gym Squash	23	2	10	Tennis balls/Solid wooden bats	In		10	25
Softball	23	18	18	Softball/Bat/Boxes		Out	20	40-50
Rider & Horse Tug o'War	25	8	40	—		Out	5	10
Watch & Jump	25	10	20	Rope	In	Out	5	10
Fire and Water	26	15	40	—	In	Out	5	10
Through the Links	26	12	30	—	In	Out	10	15
Boat Race Relay	28	8	50	—	In	Out	5	10
Team-Carrying Relay	29	8	50	—		Out	5	10
Tunnel Relay	29	12	50	—	In	Out	5	10
Joining-on Relay	30	8	50	—	In	Out	5	10
Wheel Relay	30	16	50	—		Out	5	15
Parlaauf Relay	31	8	50	—	In	Out	5	10
Serpent Relay	31	8	50	—	In	Out	5	10
Centipede Relay	32	8	50	—	In	Out	5	10
Shoulder/Grasp Relay	32	8	50	—	In	Out	5	10
Chain Relay	32	8	50	—	In	Out	5	10
Lifting Relay	32	8	50	—	In	Out	5	10
Pole Relay	33	8	30	Pole	In	Out	5	10
Bench Relay	33	8	40	Bench	In	Out	5	10
Time Ball	34	12	40	Ball	In	Out	5	15
Ball-Carrying Relay	34	8	50	Ball	In	Out	5	15
Corner Spry	35	12	40	Ball	In	Out	5	10
Down & Back Relay	35	12	50	Ball	In	Out	5	10
Pick-up Pass Relay	35	12	50	Ball	In	Out	5	15
Skittle Slalom Relay	36	10	40	Skittles	In	Out	10	15
Wall-Bounce Relay	37	10	40	One ball per team	In		10	15
Rugby Circuit	44	10	16	High jump mat, Rugby balls, Bench, Buck/Horse	In		15	30
Soccer Circuit	44	10	30	Four obstacles (skittles, balls, chairs). Bench, footballs, fixed beam	In		15	30
Athletics Circuit	46	1	40	Skipping rope, Medicine Ball, Wallbars, Boxes, Rings, Net	In		15	25
Hockey Circuit	49	12	30	Cones, Hockey balls & sticks	In	Out	10	20
Volleyball Circuit	50	12	30	Volleyballs, mats	In	Out	10	20
Basketball Circuit	51	12	30	Basketballs, Basketball ring	In		10	20
Netball Circuit	52	12	30	Benches, boxes, netballs	In	Out	10	20
Pursuit Race	54	10	50	—		Out	3	5

Game	Page	Players		Equipment	Location		Duration	
		Min.	Max.		In	Out	Min.	Max.
Obstacle Course Relay	55	10	30	4-6 High-jump mats, 2 Steeplechase barriers, 6 hurdles, 4 chairs, high jump bar, 3 benches		Out	15	30
Assorted Activities	56	30	50	Medicine Ball, beams, wallbars, box, 2 bucks	In		15	30
Backlying sprint competition	58	10	30	—		Out	5	15
Diagonal sprinting	58	10	50	4 flagposts		Out	5	10
Hops to or through the pit	58	4	15	Runway Jumping Pit		Out	10	15
Indian Trail Running	59		40/50	—		Out	5	10
Twenty-second run	59	10	40	—	In	Out	5	10
Longest & Shortest strides	59	10	40	—	In	Out	10	15
Changing Direction	59	10	40	—		Out	5	10
Up the clock and back	60	10	30	—		Out	5	15
Continuous Relay	60	10	40	Batons		Out	5	10
Shortened Fartlek	60	10	50	—		Out	10	20
Sprint Relay on a Square	61	10	30		In	Out	5	10
Watch the Hare	61	10	20	Ball	In	Out	5	10
First to the Ball	62	10	20	Ball		Out	5	10
Chasing the Attacker	62	10	30	Ball	In	Out	10	15
Speed across the circle	63	10	40	Hockey/Soccer Ball		Out	5	15
Reaction	64	8	30	Balls		Out	10	15
Pass and Squat Relay	64	10	40	Ball	In	Out	5	15
Hurdle Relay	64	10	30	Hurdles/Ball		Out	10	20
All against All	65	10	50	Tennis Balls	In		10	20
Simple Keeping it up	66	10	20	—	In	Out	5	15
Numbers from Left and Right	66	10	20	Ball and goal	In	Out	5	15
Speed Passing	67	10	20	—	In	Out	5	10
Head Handball	68	12	16	Soccer ball	In	Out	10	30
Soccer Tennis	69	8	12	Light plastic ball, net	In		10	30
Crab Football	70	12	16	Ball Goal posts	In	Out	10	20
Touch Rugby	70	10	20	4 corner flags, ball		Out	10	20
Team-Carrying Soccer	71	10	20	Ball		Out	5	10
Mobile Goal Game	71	10	20	Goalpost	In	Out	5	15
Five-a-Side Soccer using a Rugby Ball	72	10	10	Goal posts, ball	In	Out	10	20
Bench basketball	72	8	16	Basketball/netball, 2 benches	In	Out	10	20
Bouncer Handball	72	8	12	Mouldmaster/heavy plastic ball, goal posts	In	Out	10	30
Possession Ball	73	10	20	Ball	In	Out	5	15
Seven versus Five Netball	73	12	36	Netballs	In	Out	10	15
Passing and Shooting Practice	73	10	14	Net, ball	In	Out	10	30

Checklist 2
Minor Games

Game No.	Page No.	Athletics	Badminton	Basketball	Cricket	Handball	Hockey	Netball	Rounders	Rugby	Soccer	Squash	Tennis	Volleyball
1	15			✔		✔		✔		✔				
2	16			✔	✔	✔		✔		✔				
3	16			✔		✔		✔		✔				
4	17	✔		✔		✔		✔		✔	✔			
5	17	✔		✔		✔		✔		✔	✔		✔	✔
6	18				✔				✔					
7	19			✔	✔	✔		✔	✔	✔	✔			✔
8	19			✔		✔		✔		✔				
9	20			✔						✔				
10	21				✔				✔					
11	21				✔				✔					
12	21	✔		✔		✔		✔		✔				
13	22	✔		✔		✔		✔		✔	✔			
14	22		✔										✔	✔
15	23											✔	✔	
16	23				✔				✔					
17	25	✔		✔						✔	✔			✔
18	25			✔						✔				
19	26	✔	✔		✔					✔	✔			✔
20	26			✔			✔		✔	✔	✔			

Relays

Game No.	Page No.	Athletics	Badminton	Basketball	Cricket	Handball	Hockey	Netball	Rounders	Rugby	Soccer	Squash	Tennis	Volleyball
1	28	✔	✔	✔		✔		✔		✔	✔			✔
2	29	✔		✔		✔	✔	✔		✔	✔	✔	✔	✔
3	29			✔				✔		✔				
4	30	✔												
5	30	✔												

Checklist 2 continued
Relays continued

Game No.	Page No.	Athletics	Badminton	Basketball	Cricket	Handball	Hockey	Netball	Rounders	Rugby	Soccer	Squash	Tennis	Volleyball
6	31	✔	✔	✔		✔	✔	✔		✔	✔		✔	✔
7	31													
8	32													
9	32													
10	32													
11	32									✔				
12	33	✔								✔	✔			
13	33	✔					✔			✔	✔			✔
14	34			✔		✔		✔						
15	34			✔	✔	✔		✔						
16	35			✔	✔	✔		✔						
17	35	✔		✔		✔		✔		✔				
18	35									✔				
19	36	✔		✔		✔	✔	✔		✔	✔			✔
20	37			✔	✔	✔		✔	✔					

Circuits

Game No.	Page No.	Athletics	Badminton	Basketball	Cricket	Handball	Hockey	Netball	Rounders	Rugby	Soccer	Squash	Tennis	Volleyball
1	44									✔				
2	44										✔			
3	46	✔							✔					
4	49						✔							
5	50													✔
6	51			✔										
7	52							✔						

Activities Relating to Major Games

Game No.	Page No.	Athletics	Badminton	Basketball	Cricket	Handball	Hockey	Netball	Rounders	Rugby	Soccer	Squash	Tennis	Volleyball
1	54	✔	✔	✔	✔	✔	✔	✔	✔	✔	✔	✔	✔	✔
2	55	✔												
3	56	✔		✔	✔	✔		✔	✔	✔	✔	✔	✔	✔
4	58	✔												
5	58	✔		✔						✔	✔			

Checklist 2 continued
Activities Relating to Major Games continued

Game No.	Page No.	Athletics	Badminton	Basketball	Cricket	Handball	Hockey	Netball	Rounders	Rugby	Soccer	Squash	Tennis	Volleyball
6	58	✔		✔						✔	✔			✔
7	59	✔					✔	✔		✔	✔			
8	59	✔		✔			✔	✔		✔	✔		✔	
9	59	✔		✔			✔	✔		✔	✔		✔	✔
10	59	✔		✔		✔			✔	✔	✔	✔	✔	✔
11	60	✔		✔		✔	✔	✔		✔	✔			
12	60	✔												
13	60	✔		✔	✔	✔	✔	✔		✔	✔	✔	✔	✔
14	61	✔		✔		✔	✔	✔		✔	✔		✔	

Skill Practice Games

Game No.	Page No.	Athletics	Badminton	Basketball	Cricket	Handball	Hockey	Netball	Rounders	Rugby	Soccer	Squash	Tennis	Volleyball
1	61	✔	✔	✔	✔	✔	✔	✔	✔	✔	✔	✔	✔	✔
2	62	✔	✔	✔	✔	✔	✔	✔	✔	✔	✔	✔	✔	✔
3	62			✔			✔		✔	✔	✔			
4	63						✔			✔				
5	64	✔	✔	✔	✔	✔		✔	✔	✔	✔	✔	✔	✔
6	64													
7	64		✔	✔	✔		✔	✔	✔		✔			✔
8	65			✔						✔	✔			
9	66										✔			✔
10	66										✔			✔
11	67			✔		✔	✔	✔		✔	✔			

Mini Games

Game No.	Page No.	Athletics	Badminton	Basketball	Cricket	Handball	Hockey	Netball	Rounders	Rugby	Soccer	Squash	Tennis	Volleyball
1	68		✔			✔				✔	✔			
2	69										✔			
3	70									✔	✔			
4	70									✔				
5	71										✔			
6	71			✔		✔	✔	✔			✔			

Checklist 2 continued
Mini Games continued

Game No.	Page No.	Athletics	Badminton	Basketball	Cricket	Handball	Hockey	Netball	Rounders	Rugby	Soccer	Squash	Tennis	Volleyball
7	72									✔	✔			
8	72			✔				✔						
9	72			✔		✔		✔						
10	73			✔		✔		✔		✔				
11	73							✔						
12	73			✔				✔						